Around the isles . . .

D1643016

THE SOUTH ISLES

1. St Margaret's Hope.
2. Festival of the horse.
3. Italian Chapel, Lamb Holm.
4. Italian Chapel.
5. No. 3 Churchill Barrier.
6. Copinsay Lighthouse.
7. Martello Tower, South Walls.
8. Kirk Hope, Hoy.
9. Rackwick, Hoy.
10. Brig over Pegal Burn, Hoy.
11. *St Ola* going out around Hoy.
12. The Old Man of Hoy.
13. Wreck of the *Inverlane*, Burra Sound
14. Hoy Sound.

KIRKWALL

15. Aerial view of Kirkwall.
16. "Otters crossing", Kirkwall.
17. St Magnus Cathedral, Kirkwall.
18. St Magnus Cathedral, Kirkwall.
19. Broad Street, Kirkwall.
20. Main Street, Kirkwall.
21. The Bishop's Palace, Kirkwall.
22. The Earl's Palace, Kirkwall.
23. Tankerness House, Kirkwall.
24. Kirkwall harbour.

STROMNESS

25. Stromness harbour.
26. Stromness harbour.
27. Stromness waterfront.
28. Stromness.
29. Login's Well, Stromness.
30. Stromness — South End by night.

MAINLAND

31. Yesnaby Castle.
32. Stack of Yesnaby.
33. Skara Brae.
34. Rough Seas, Yesnaby.
35. Kitchener's Memorial, Marwick Head.
36. An Orkney Garden.
37. Scapa pier.
38. Sunset, Scapa beach.
39. Bigging district, Rendall.
40. Foot of Heddle Road, Firth.
41. Click Mill, Dounby.

42. *Harray*
43. Brough of Birsay.
44. Loch of Harray.
45. Tormiston Mill, Stenness.
46. Burn of Heddle, Stenness.
47. The Ring of Brodgar.
48. Mill of Eyrland, Stenness.
49. Winter scene.
50. Orphir and Hoy hills.
51. Threshing oats.

THE NORTH ISLES

52. Whitehall village, Stronsay.
53. Dishan Tower, Shapinsay.
54. Balfour Castle, Shapinsay.
55. St Magnus Church, Egilsay.
56. Hullion, Rousay.
57. Kettletoft, Sanday.
58. Kettletoft, Sanday.
59. Harvest Scene, Papa Westray.
60. Fowl Craig, Papa Westray.
61. Fishing boats, North Ronaldsay.
62. North Ronaldsay sheep.
63. Croft at Aith.

1. The picturesque village of St Margaret's Hope, South Ronaldsay. © *M. Richardson, 1990*.

2. The Festival of the Horse is celebrated in St Margaret's Hope every August. © *P. & V. Reynolds, 1990.*

3. The Italian Chapel, Lamb Holm, constructed by Italian prisoners of war during the Second World War. The chapel was designed by Domenico Chiocchetti, in peacetime an artist and church decorator. © *James Weir, 1987.*

4. The Italian Chapel.

© M. Moar, 1991.

5.   No. 3 Churchill Barrier linking Glims Holm to Burray. The Churchill Barriers were built during the Second World War to seal the eastern approaches to Scapa Flow. © *D. Copland, 1990.*

6. Copinsay Lighthouse.   © *M. Richardson, 1989.*

7. Martello Gun Tower, South Walls, built for protection during the Napoleonic Wars. © R. Wilson, 1991.

8.   Kirk Hope, Hoy.

© R. S. Moore, 1989.

9. Rackwick, Hoy, from Moor Fea.

10. Brig over Pegal Burn, Hoy.

© *D. Copland, 1990.*

11.   The *St Ola*, which crosses the Pentland Firth several times daily linking Orkney to the Mainland of Scotland, going out around Hoy.   © *R. Welsby, 1992*.

12.   The Old Man of Hoy, a 450' sandstone sea stack.   © *James Weir, 1987.*

13. Wreck of the *Inverlane*, Burra Sound.

14 Hoy Sound.

15.   Aerial view of Kirkwall, Orkney's capital city. St Magnus Cathedral can be seen to the left of the foreground.

16.   Otters are regularly seen crossing at the Ayre Mills, Kirkwall.

© *P. & V. Reynolds, 1990.*

17. St Magnus Cathedral, Kirkwall, founded in 1137 and constructed of rich, red sandstone. The remains of St Magnus lie in the north choir pillar.

© *James Weir, 1987.*

18. St Magnus Cathedral, Kirkwall.

© *M. Richardson, 1989*.

19. Broad Street, Kirkwall.

20.	The "big tree" on Main Street, Kirkwall. Not long after this view was published in our 1987 calendar the tree was drastically pruned.

© *James Weir, 1987.*

21.   The Bishop's Palace, Kirkwall. King Hakon died here in 1263 after his defeat at the Battle of Largs.

22.   The Earl's Palace, Kirkwall, built by Earl Patrick Stewart in 1607.   © *James Weir, 1987.*

23. Tankerness House, Kirkwall, now the town's museum. © M. Edwards, 1991.

24. Kirkwall Harbour, the scene of recent expansion. © *James Weir, 1988.*

25.   Stromness harbour. The town shelters beneath Brinkies' Brae.

26. Norwegian sailing ship *Sørlandet* in Stromness.   © *W. Hancox, 1990.*

27. Stromness waterfront with the P&O Ferries berth in the background. The large pier in the foreground is the Lighthouse Pier which used to be the base for the lighthouse ship *Pole Star*.

28.   Stromness with the modern building of Stromness Primary School in the centre. The tourist office is on the right at the top of the pier.

© R. Baikie, 1991.

LOGIN'S WELL

THERE WATERED HERE
THE HUDSON BAY COY'S SHIPS
1670 - 1891
CAPT. COOK'S VESSELS
RESOLUTION AND DISCOVERY
1780
SIR JOHN FRANKLIN'S SHIPS
EREBUS AND TERROR
ON ARCTIC EXPLORATION
1845
ALSO THE MERCHANT VESSELS
OF FORMER DAYS

WELL SEALED UP 1931

29. Login's Well, Stromness. Although this well was sealed in 1931 the inscription reveals some of the nautical history of Stromness. During the last century many ships stopped at Stromness to take on water before setting sail for Hudson Bay. *© James Weir, 1988.*

30.   Stromness — South End by night.

31. Yesnaby Castle, a dramatic sea stack on Orkney's Atlantic coastline.

32. Stack of Yesnaby.

33. Skara Brae, Sandwick, a neolithic stone village dating from 3000 BC. © *James Weir, 1987.*

34. Rough Seas, Yesnaby.

© R. Welsby, 1992.

35. Kitchener's Memorial, Marwick Head. Built to commemorate the loss in 1916 of HMS *Hampshire* and Lord Kitchener, Minister of War.

© *James Weir, 1988.*

36. An Orkney garden. © *James Weir, 1988.*

37. Scapa pier.

38. Sunset, Scapa beach.

© M. Sinclair, 1992.

39. Bigging district, Rendall.

40.   Foot of Heddle Road, Firth.

41. Click Mill, Dounby. A horizontal watermill, called after the noise made while working, and the last of its kind in Orkney.

42. Corigall Farm Museum, Harray, a restored 19th century farmstead. © *James Weir, 1988.*

43. Standing Stone, Brough of Birsay.   © *G. Wallington, 1991.*

44. Loch of Harray.

45. Tormiston Mill, Stenness. A three-storey meal mill now converted into a craft shop and restaurant.

46. Burn of Heddle and Tormiston Mill, Stenness.

47. The Ring of Brodgar, a wide circle of standing stones situated on the Ness of Brodgar. © *James Weir, 1987.*

48. Mill of Eyrland, Stenness.

49. Winter scene.

50. Orphir and Hoy hills.

51. Threshing oats.

52. High tide, Whitehall village, Stronsay.

© I. Cooper, 1992.

53.   The Dishan Tower, Shapinsay, originally a dovecot, guards the entrance to Elwick Bay. © *M. Horrie, 1992.*

54. Baronial-style Balfour Castle on Shapinsay overlooking the Bay of Elwick. © *P. & V. Reynolds, 1990.*

55. St Magnus Church, Egilsay, with its cylindrical tower at the west end.   © *K. Pirie, 1991.*

56. Hullion, Rousay.

© R. Baikie, 1991.

57. 'Steamer day', Kettletoft, Sanday.

58. Kettletoft, Sanday.

59. Harvest Scene, Papa Westray.

© *M. Cooper, 1990.*

60. Fowl Craig, Papa Westray, with its colony of seabirds.

© *M. Cooper, 1990.*

61. Fishing boats, North Ronaldsay.

62. North Ronaldsay sheep. The island is surrounded by a 6' high drystane dyke to keep the native sheep, who
live mainly on seaweed, off the cultivated land. © *P. & V. Reynolds, 1992.*

63. Croft at Aith.

© James Weir, 1987.